White aster : a Japanese epic; together with other poems from the German adaptation of Prof. Dr. Karl Florenz

Karl Florenz, Tetsujiro Inoue

WHITE ASTER
A JAPANESE EPIC

TOGETHER WITH
OTHER POEMS

from the German Adaptation of

Prof. Dr. Karl Florenz

By

A. Lloyd, M.A.

Published by

T. Hasegawa

'O Hiyoshicho, Tokyo, Jap

DEDICATED
AS A TOKEN OF GRATITUDE
AND RESPECT
TO
GEORGE EBERS

PREFACE.

Long epics are of rare occurrence in Japanese literature as in Chinese, and the few specimens in existence
scarcely deserve to be ranked with our western
epopees. Little stress is laid on plot or development
of action: characters with very marked features seldom
present themselves, and there is very little attempt to
penetrate into the unfathomable depths of human pas-
sions. On the other hand, they are rich in pictures
and in descriptions of natural phenomena: no sooner
has the poet briefly touched upon the inward conflict
of the heart, than he lets his fancy turn back at once
to the visible things of the world, which he takes
pleasure in describing with great rhetorical skill. In
the version which is here offered to the favorable

consideration of the western reader the translator has allowed himself considerable latitude, sometimes trying to render his original accurately, and sometimes very freely; thinking that he could thus do more justice to the poets of the Far East than he could by a rigidly conscientious literal translation which would have killed all the poetical charm of the work.

"White Aster" came before the German translator in two forms. He consulted it in its Chinese original under the title of 孝女白菊の詩, "the Lay of the Pious Maiden Shirakiku" (i. e. White Aster), as composed by the great Sinologue Professor *Tetsujiro Inouye*; but he also had before him a rendering of this poem into classical Japanese by the eminent scholar Naobumi Ochiai (孝女白菊の歌).

Ochiai's rendering is much prized in Japanese literary circles on account of its masterly handing of the language, but to our taste Inouye's original is richer in delicate shades of thought, and the translator has therefore based his own rendering exclusively on this one. We beg therefore to offer to our readers a work in which the situations and the personages, the action and the sentiment, are all Japanese, though tinged with Chinese art and rhetoric,—always premising that every translation (and how much more does this apply to the English version!) is like silver—one always loses by the exchange.

The illustrations to this book have been designed and executed by two Japanese artists. The greater part come from the pencil of *Mishima Yunosuke,* (三島雄之助;—known in art as 蕉窓 *Shosō*), who designed the cover, and pp 1-71; *Arai Shujiro* (新井周次郎. art-name, *Yoshimune* 芳宗) is responsible only for the illustrations to the smaller poems, pp 72-80.

Tokyo, Autumn of 1895.

(German Edition)　　　　Prof. Dr. K. Florenz.

Autumn of 1897.

(English Edition)　　　　A. Lloyd. M. A.

CANTO I.

The sun went down, and its last level rays,
As with a golden veil of mist, enveloping
The mount of Aso, lay upon the thorp.
The wind with gentle murmurs through the trees,
Scattered the many-tinted Autumn leaves,
Like pattering raindrops, countless on the earth.

Just then, within the distant temple-grove,
Boomed forth the deep notes of a smitten bell;
When from a hut that stood upon the fringe
And outskirts of the village, crept a maid,
Straining her eyes to scan the Autumn fields,
And as she gazed, upon each eager lid
Sparkled a teardrop, that no loved one came,
That thus she stood looking abroad in vain,
The solitary inmate of the hut.

For now three weary days had dragged away
Since that her sire had climbed the mountain side
And not returned. At early dawn he went,
Shouldering his hunting nets and trusty gun,
Across the slushy fields, and where the wind
Breathed through the rustling reed-grass, whilst the moon,
Pale with its latest conflict with the dawn,
Beamed faintly o'er the temple's hallowed roof.
Thence, by the path that leads towards the hill,
He climbed, and quickly disappeared from sight.

Then even fell — but he came not; and night
Fell, gloom'd, and broke; and once more days and nights
Passed, — yet he never came. Then she in fear,
Dreading mishap, enquired everywhere
From friends and neighbours; — None had seen
His traces,

And so now her tearful eye
Wandered in vain over the outspread scene,

Mists, cold and dark, were rising slowly up,
And with their mantle grey were wrapping o'er
The silken carpet of red maple leaves.
Then darkness fell: and gathering the dry leaves,
Wind–blown, that lay in ridges all around,
She kindles on the hearth a crackling fire,
Handles the fan with deftly moving wrist,
Awakes the slumbering gleed within the coals,
And boils the kettle for the evening tea.

4

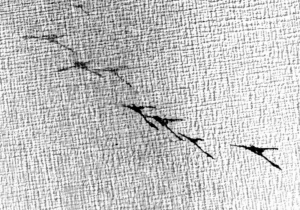

Meantime the door oft rattles, and each time
She starts, thinking "'Tis Father"—; but the wind
Was mocking her with idle rappings. Thus
Hours long she sat, and with her grieving eye
Gazed now upon the glowing fire, and now
Upon the rising clouds of steam that danced
Fantastic right across the darkening room,
Like those sweet dreams that fill a man with hope,
And, gaily dancing, sink to nothingness.
Deep sunk in sleep lay all the villagers,
And all around was solitary still,
Save where across the clouded heavens moved,
With mournful cries, flocks of belated geese.
    The sky had changed its dress, and suddenly
Wrapped round itself a cloak of black rain clouds:
Noisily shrilled the cold autumnal blast,
Bowed low the leaves, ducking, as though in fear,
And loudly storming fell the rain to earth.

White-Aster heard it, shuddering, and with pain
Thought of her father's suffering (who can tell?):
Nor longer, thus inactive, can she bear
To hear the rain splash, and the howling wind
With patience. Hastily resolved, she throws
Her blue cloak o'er her shoulder; on her head,
A hat of red bamboo, and thus goes forth
Adown the village-street and from the street,
Through field and bush and grove, towards the hills.
Here the steep path winds with a swift ascent
Towards the summit:—the long grass that grew
In tufts upon the slopes, shrivelled and dry,
Lay dead upon her path—; hushed was the voice
Of the blithe chafers — Only sable night

Yawned threatening from the vale. Nor voice of man,
Nor cry of beast, gives token of a life
Existing in the waste. The wind alone
Howls in the cypresses and rocking pines,
With roaring voice, as of the storm-thrashed waves.
Then by degrees the downpour ceased,—and lo!
The sombre veil of clouds was rent, and through
The widening rifts peered out the moon and stars,
To find a mirror in the crystal stream,
That glided smoothly o'er its bed of rock.

Now to a bridge she came, that, built of stone,
Stood hoar with mossy age, and crossing it
Followed the crooked path against the stream,
That rushed down chattering to his rocky friends.
Where should she seek the footsteps of her sire?

Salt tears of anguish rose, and from her eyes
Flowed, in a copious stream, adown her cheeks,
Staining the sleeves that strove to stem their flood.
So roamed she aimless, up and down the hills,
Until, at length, within a little grove
The narrow path was lost. But in the grove,
O'er-shadowed by the gloomy cypresses
And branching camphor-trees, she spied from far
A temple, and a voice come thro' the air,
As of a priest intoning on his book.

8

Bleached bones lay on the ground, and rows of graves
Stood like gray ghosts; with downward stretching arms
The weeping willows kissed the impure earth
That breathed corruption; mouldering stood the roof;
The rotten pillars stood aslant; the wind
Piped through the broken paper window panes,
Through which there gleamed a faintly glimmering light.
Pushing aside the wanton-growing hedge,
She stumbled up the broken steps of stone

That lead within the silent temple-yard:
The moonlight shining on her through the trees,
Tinted her face with its own ghostly hue.

But when the anchorite within perceived
The sound of steps, he rose up from his desk,
Candle in hand, half-opening the crank door,
And saw a shadow moving o'er the ground.
Then feared he, and his face grew ashy pale:
"Avaunt! fox-ghost," he cried; "Thou mock'st me not;
"No tender maid of human birth would thus
Brave the wild humours of this stormy night."
To whom, with gently pleading voice, the maid:

"I am a poor and solitary maid:
No spirit I, that with deceitful charms
Draws near to lure thee to perdition foul.
Be not alarmed that I thus all alone,
At such an hour, should break upon thy peace:
I seek my father on these mountain tracts;
And therefore wander thus o'er desert paths."

10

So spake she. As with modest mien she stood
Thus before him in homely country dress,
All unadorned, save with pure Nature's grace,
What man her beauty's charms could have resisted?
" 'Tis clear she comes of noble family:
Her eyebrows are as twin half moons: her hair
Lies on her snowy temples, like a cloud:
In charm of form she ranks with Sishih's self,
That pearl of loveliness, the Chinese Helen."

Wondering, the monk fixed his dark eye on her
And asked, astonished, " Maiden, whence art thou?"
Much of her story was he fain to ask,
Yet first he led the maid within the shrine,
And bade her sit before the sanctuary.

Shrieked through the broken panes the mountain wind,
Flickered the dull flame in the dingy lamp,
Black pitchy darkness filled the empty hall,
Save where the lamplight on the idols fell.
Without, a brook was rushing down the rocks,
With noise that pierced the flimsy walls, the bats
Flew to and fro, and their dark-wandering wings
With light breath touched her hands and weary cheeks.

At Buddha's feet the maiden sat and dried
Her moistened eyes, from which the copious tears
Flowed silent down her cheeks, and, with forced calm,
Thus to the monk began her mournful tale:
    I am the daughter of a Samurai:
Where the famed towers of Kumamoto raise
Their proud heads heavenward, in the southern isle,
There was I cradled — in a stately house,
Richly set out, with costly palanquins,
And neighing steeds, pure bred; abundant stores
Of toothsome dainties for all appetites.
No sad mischance befalling e'er disturbed
Our home's perennial peace: — with equal ray,
Warming and bright, the friendly sun beheld

Our broad verandah, gay with velvet tints
Of blooming peonies — and hanging blinds
Of rushes, bound with silk, softened the glare
That blazed too fiercely in the summer noon,

    Here dreamed I my young life, foreboding ill.
Then suddenly the sounds of warfare filled
The land, — soldiers were marching — and the dust
Of combat, rising, darkened all the air.
But few escaped the all-devouring death
That drank the life-blood of the country, and
Incarnadined the fields with streams of blood.
Strewed with the whitening bones of slaughtered men
The battle-fields were marked, — on all sides round,
Ruined and charred, the barns and homesteads stood
Black monuments of war ; — while shrieking crows
Flying in thousands o'er the desert roads
Swooped down to forage. Young and old alike
Fled, leaving home and fields and goods,
In panic-stricken troops, from where the foe,
Stood round the moated castle. 'Twas no time
For dangerous hesitancy : I, too, fled,
So did my mother, and with her I sought
A sheltering refuge. The cold Autumn wind
Blew, and the leaves fell countless, when one eve
We spied an ancient temple. Overhead,

The sky was clear, and, with a waning light,
The moon's last sickle-crescent glimmering forth
Lit up a wasted plain, and in its midst
A ruined village — whose deserted street
(Nor man nor beast was there, nor any sound)
Made waste more woful.   Here we sought
A temporary shelter and a place
To shield us from the wind: a wretched roof
We wove of reeds and rushes formed our home,
And thus in need and misery we staid
There at the foot of Aso.   My own hands
Supplied our scanty wants — water and wood,
For warmth and food —, to drag out painful day
That like the night-mare's horrors, slowly crept.

    Yet worse remained in store, the cup of woe
Was not yet drained, — for suddenly we heard
That joining with the rebel bands, my sire
Had fought against the King, — the sad revolt
Had now been crushed, and all the rebel lords
Justly condemned to death —: one bloody fight

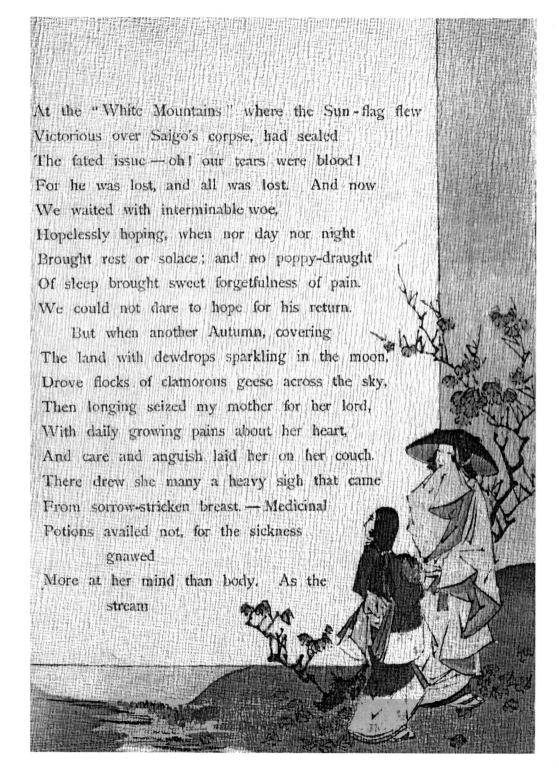

At the "White Mountains" where the Sun-flag flew
Victorious over Saigo's corpse, had sealed
The fated issue — oh! our tears were blood!
For he was lost, and all was lost.   And now
We waited with interminable woe,
Hopelessly hoping, when nor day nor night
Brought rest or solace; and no poppy-draught
Of sleep brought sweet forgetfulness of pain.
We could not dare to hope for his return.
      But when another Autumn, covering
The land with dewdrops sparkling in the moon,
Drove flocks of clamorous geese across the sky,
Then longing seized my mother for her lord,
With daily growing pains about her heart,
And care and anguish laid her on her couch.
There drew she many a heavy sigh that came
From sorrow-stricken breast. — Medicinal
Potions availed not, for the sickness
      gnawed
More at her mind than body.   As the
      stream

Flows to the sea and nevermore returns,
So ebbed and ebbed her life. I cannot tell
What in those days I suffered.   Nature's self
Seemed to be mourning with me, for the breeze
Of Autumn breathed its last, and as it died
The Vesper-bell from yonder village pealed
A requiem o'er my mother. Thus she died,
But dead yet lives — for, ever, face and form,
She stands before my eyes; and in my ears
I ever seem to hear her loving voice,
Speaking as in the days when, strict and kind,
She thought me household lore, — in all a mother.
Ah! could I but with some light act repay
Her mother-love so rich and manifold!
Deeply I grieve, and with deep shame confess
That I have never loved her as I ought.
I see the story of my woe has touched
Your heart, yet list, and, listening, feel the joy
That filled my breast. For last year, suddenly,
He whom we wept as dead, my father, came
To seek and save us. Adverse circumstance
Had driven him here and there, until at last
He dared once more to show his face at home.

Ah! many were the tears I saw him shed,
As I related all the mournful tale
Of mother's death; and yet with words of love
I tried all arts of filial blandishment
To soothe his grief, and in some wise replace
Her whom he lost:—Henceforth at every hour
My sole endeavour was to clear the clouds
Of melancholy brooding on his brow.
And now a few days since, ere yet the dawn
Had fully broke, he took his nets and gun
And went towards the mountains, there to hunt.
Three days in vain I wait for his return;
The neighbours have not seen a trace of him:
We know not — has he lost the narrow path
Among the wooded rocks? or from a cliff
Fall'n into a ravine? Ah! thousandfold
Fear seizes me and anguish, nor have I
Any to counsel with me and advise!
Thus have I come alone to seek him here,
Myself, through all this storm. But
        you, good sir,
Shrink not from one bowed down by
        need, nor think

You see a trickish mountain spirit here.
White - Aster is my name, born of the race
Of Honda; Akitoshi is my sire,
O - Take is my mother, relatives
I have in plenty — but for many a day
I have not seen them. The rebellion
Scattered them as the whirlwind does the leaves
That fall in Autumn. Solitary, lone,
You see me stand before you, and the future
Has nought in store for me. I had a brother;
His name was Akihide, but his nature
Was wild and overbearing, and my father
Longsuffering as he was, at last lost patience
And drove him forth in anger; nor know I
What has become of him: perhaps he's dead."
At this the recluse flushed and then grew pale,
And in his breast an ill-restrained sigh
Gave token of a raging storm within,

Where feeling strove with feeling: yet he kept
His self-restraint in silence. Monk and maid
Facing each other sat, as though quite lost
In dreams of dark foreboding. In her eyes
Then glanced a shining teardrop: but the monk
Veiled with his outspread hands his anguished face.

    At last, he broke the silence, and upraised
His gentle eyes, and spoke with kindly voice:
"As long as it is night, you must not think
To trust yourself to these inclement hills;
Stay here, I pray, till then: it is not safe
To wander now. Stay, till the wakeful cock
Proclaims the dawn, and in the gathering light
The eastward hills grow red: the rising sun
Shall bring new joy and lighten all your path."

    Thus spake he, and she felt how kind and wise
The words were that he spoke, and, silently
Consenting, laid her down before the shrine

To slumber. But her rest was much disturbed;
For, her thin robes ill sheltering her limbs,
She froze e'en as she slept. Her weary head
Was filled with dreams; for, lo! with tearful eyes,
And solemn countenance, her father stood
Close by her pillow. "One false step," he cried,
Hurled me into a deep ravine, where now
Thick brushwood holds me that I cannot move
Forwards, nor backwards. Thus three weary days
I've suffered: thirst and hunger fill my frame
With martyr-pains of hell, till in despair
I pray that I may lose my wretched life.

Whiteaster rose, striving to catch his coat,
And question further; but he vanished
Quick as he came, and left no trace behind.

The night was still: no sound fell on the ear,
The Temple slept in peace, save here and there
A gentle breeze up-springing moved the crowns
Of jewelled bamboo-stems, that answering
Rustled with gentle whispers. Thus the night
Passed, and the moonlight faded, and the panes
Began to gleam, as through them, westward, passed
The first faint glimmers of the orient day.

CANTO II.

Now the red dawn had tipped the mountain
tops,
And birds, awaking, peered from out their
nests,
To greet the day with strains of matin joy;
The while the moon's pale sickle, silver
white,
Fading away, sunk in the western sky.
Clear was the air and cloudless, save the
mists
That rolled in waves upon the mountain
tops,
Or crept along the gullies. Here the maid

Took leave of
the recluse,
and sped
her way
Through the bright morn,
along the rocky
path
Adorned with grass
and flowers.
The rising sun,
With level rays of
fiery glamour,
cast
Her ghostlike shadow on the ruined wall
Of an old broken house: then, as she went,
With tongues of flame it passed betwixt the
clouds,
And flooded with a sea of golden light
Forests and clouds, mountains and happy
vales.

Once more her path lay under mighty trees
That stood, as giant watchmen, over her,
And made her shudder, as the mountain wind
Stirred in their tops, and woke the whispering pines
That, ghostlike, shook their heads, and dropping down
Their sharp green needles, touched her conscious
        sleeve.
All else was silent, for no human soul
Breathed in this solitude; — her very step
Died echoless upon the mossy floor.
Now, stooping, would she pluck a tiny flower
That blossomed by her path, now, standing still,
Listen to hear the silence. One white cloud
Raced with her o'er the heights, and often seemed
To seize her dress and carry her away.
Birds rocked upon the branches as she passed,
Unknown in voice and plumage: all around,
The scene was strange   and unfamiliar.

          he clearing stands a herd of deer,
Seeking refreshment in the icy stream,
Which, like a truthful mirror, still reflects
The sheen of yonder maples, which the frosts
Have not yet robbed of their autumnal charms.
Far as the eye can reach, mountains and hills,
Mountains and deep-sunk valleys, and a fringe
Of dark-green woods; and, winding under them,
The road to Hoshu passes out of sight.

          And where is now her father? Ah! no trace
Shows where he passed, and all the many charms
Of much adorned Nature seem to mock
Her grieving heart, and, as she hurries on,
The forest-stillness seems to laugh at her.
But, look, those dark forms creeping after her,
With cruel speed, and, with discourteous hands,
Seizing the shrinking maiden—who are they?
Robbers they are, who seize her as their prey,
And lead her hastily, with cruel force,
O'er stocks and stones, to their ungodly den.
In piteous distress, she now 'gins cry,
Screaming for help;—no friendly knight is near,
And only Echo answers to her call.

Quickly they brought her where a thicket dense
Concealed the entrance to a dark ravine,
At which the robbers, and their helpless prey,
Plunged in and disappeared. In this recess,
Lay a recess more secret. 'Neath a rock,
Like gable-tree projecting from its base,
Stood, half in ruins, a low-constructed house.
The broken reed-thatch scarce could bear th' attacks
Of wind and rain; but thick-grown ginko trees,
Which, like to golden clouds, filled the ravine,
Saved the scant thatch. A ceaseless chattering brook
Flowed by the house, and the rank ivy-stems
Grew o'er the broken windows. Here the sun
Ne'er visits with his parting rays at eve,
But all is gloom and silence save the cry
Of some belated bird that wakes the night.
Here with wild shouts, because their prize was rare,
The robbers called their comrades, who received
Them and their captive with much boisterous joy,
Putting a thousand questions to the maid,
Who wept, and almost fainted in her fear.
Then with coarse jests they mocked her, as the crows
That scold at carrion. Then they sat them down,

All in a circle, to the joyful feast.
The saké-cask was broached; and smoke-dried fish,
Mountains of pork, with rice and radishes,
Were piled in bowls and dishes. They, despising
The chop-sticks' cleanly offices, put forth
Their hands to grasp the food, and, like wild wolves,
Ate noisily their fill, with greedy haste,
And much lip-smacking at the abundant cheer.
　　Now, when their first keen greed was satisfied,
One, who seemed captain of the noisy crew,
Arose, and leering with bold lustful eyes,
Approached the modest beauty: "See," he cried,
"I am the king of this free mountain-folk:

But ne'er before has Fortune smiled on us
With gift of lovely maiden. Listen now!
For many years I've had within this house
A koto, on which no one ever yet
Has played. Now you shall be the first, to-day,
To play on it, and, with sweet melodies,
To give us longed for pleasure. Sit you down,
And let us hear your skill; for I do swear
That, if you hesitate, then with this sword
I'll cut you into bits, and give your flesh
To yonder noisy crows. Mark well my words."

    Like a sharp knife, the cruel robber's words
Pierced to her heart. But what can woman's strength
Avail against the blinded lusts of men?
So, though in heart rebellious, her soft hands
She reached out to the harp, and touched the strings
Gently at first, and feebly; then with strength
That gathered in the music. Thus she played
As ne'er she played before. For, in her heart

Excitement, passion, pain, held tournament,
And all her thoughts, and every hope and fear,—
Her inmost self—found voices in the strings.
Now, as the Fall-wind rustling in the tress,
It sounded, low and sad; and now, as though
The ghost of some poor crane from Paradise
Were hovering o'er this moon-lit world of ours,
Her grief cried shrill and weird; and then again,
As when the night rain in the bamboo-groves
By Siang's streams, patters and drips to earth.
Then voices, as of spirits, hovered o'er
The minstrel, and the sound of dropping pearls
Into a jewelled bowl, that fall and break
With clear sharp crack into a thousand bits.
No wonder were it if the river-god
Danced to her strains, and e'en the dragon-fiend,
That lurks beneath the waves, stood up to hear.

She ceased.   The darkened mountain-peaks around
Lay still and peaceful as a slumbering babe :
The moon gleamed through the broken window-panes,
The air was clear and bright.   The woods alone
Re-echoed with the music's dying strains.
E'en the harsh robbers' hearts could not withstand
The magic power of song ; — but, silently
Contemplative, they marked its waning notes,
Mindful of long forgotten piety.

Meanwhile a man, armed with sword and spear,
Had stolen to the house, and, with loud cries,
Bursting the door, attacked the festive crew
With lightning onset.   Ere the robber band,
All unprepared for combat, could begin
To rouse resistance, it was all too late,
For, like the hailstones, thick and fast, his blows
Fell, and his arm mowed opposition down,
Till but one man escaped by timely flight.
Streams of warm blood flowed trickling o'er the mats,
And stained the plates and dishes : here, the heads
Lay with their eyes still opened wide, and there,
The headless trunks lay motionless and stiff.

Who was the hero that performed this deed
Sole and unaided ? His black robe, and cap

Of silk proclaim the priest: with quiet hand,
He wiped his bloodstained sword, and called the maid
Into the doorway, where the waxing moon
Shone on his face, and thus began to speak:

    "Be without fear, White Aster: thee to save
I came: thou sawst me yesternight, and now
From my own lips shalt gather who I am;
For longer would it ill be seem to hide.
Your brother I; you gaze at me in doubt,
And muse incredulously, how the man,
Whom you remember full of wicked lusts,
Ungoverned, unrestrained, and slave to vice,
Should stand before you in a hermit's garb?
Yet listen. When my father drove me out,
Lone and forsaken, many years I spent,
In wandering, oft repentant, but my pride
Held me from seeking pardon. So I came
One spring to Yedo, and engaged myself,
Half student and half servant, in the house
Of the famed teacher Keiu, where I read
The ancient classics and the holy books,
Which as I studied deeper, and compared
My own life's conduct with the moral rules
Of the great Chinese doctor — how despised

And despicable seemed my life to be!

    Thus sat I once at eventide, and read
My book before the window — fine spring rain
Was drizzling in the garden, and the wind
Sighed in the trees. Unbearable became
The load of bitter memories; the laugh
And chatter of my comrades turned to pain:
And all the world was bitter. I resolved,
Manlike, to change my life and with the change
Return, a new man, to my father's house.

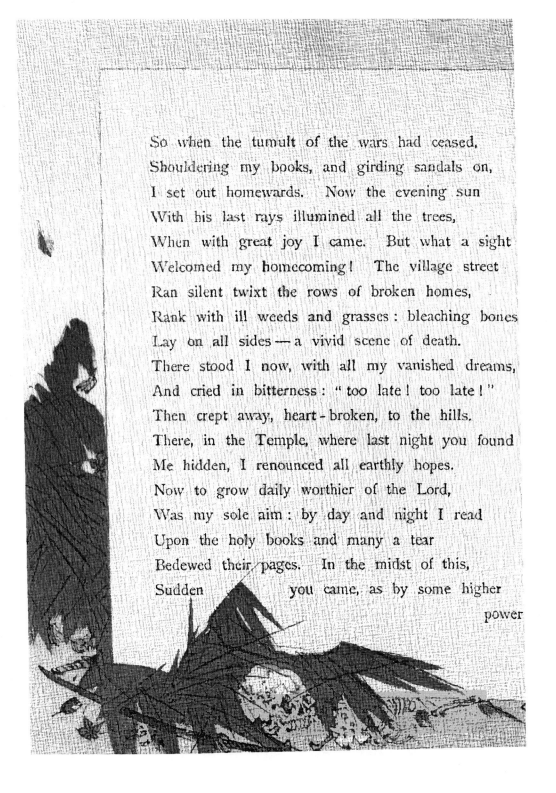

So when the tumult of the wars had ceased,
Shouldering my books, and girding sandals on,
I set out homewards. Now the evening sun
With his last rays illumined all the trees,
When with great joy I came. But what a sight
Welcomed my homecoming! The village street
Ran silent twixt the rows of broken homes,
Rank with ill weeds and grasses : bleaching bones
Lay on all sides — a vivid scene of death.
There stood I now, with all my vanished dreams,
And cried in bitterness : "too late ! too late !"
Then crept away, heart - broken, to the hills.
There, in the Temple, where last night you found
Me hidden, I renounced all earthly hopes.
Now to grow daily worthier of the Lord,
Was my sole aim : by day and night I read
Upon the holy books and many a tear
Bedewed their pages. In the midst of this,
Sudden   you came, as by some higher
                                    power

Conducted, and with deep emotion stirred
I heard you tell the fortunes of our house.
Much then my spirit fought against itself,
Wishing to tell my name and welcome you,
My long-lost sister; but false shame forbade,
And kept my mouth tight closed.   Fear undefined
Pressed on my heart this morning, when you took
Leave of me; for I knew that robber bands,
Throughout these mountains, make the paths unsafe,
So tracking you all day, I followed on,
And found you here amidst this blackguard crew.
There they lie, dead by the avenging sword,
In their own dirty blood, and you are free.
As far as the next village I will lead you,
And help you find our father: but his eyes
Shall ne'er behold me more.   On this same spot
Where I saved you, my hand shall end my life,
And self-sought death shall purge away my guilt.
So spake he; was it a confusing dream
That dazed her sense? or was it really true,

That she had found her brother? Wav'ring doubt
Was all impossible. Bright tears of joy
Gleamed in her eyes and trickling down her cheeks
Fell on her new-found brother's brawny hand.
With words of sweetest love she spoke him fair,
And breathed new hope: how oft her father had
Longed for his lost son, and with bitter grief
Killed all his former harshness. — Gathering night
Had settled on the land, whilst yet they spoke:
The frosty mountain air was crisp and clear
As running streamlets: on the zenith, stood
The silver moon; across the cloudless sky,
Some wild geese flying told the hour of night.

CANTO III.

It yet was night. — Valley and mountain lay
In deep and solemn silence: from the woods,
The long - drawn plaintive cry of monkey bands
Breaking alone the stillness. In the west,
The moon lay low upon the horizon's edge,
In act to hide behind a band of clouds.
White Aster, with her brother, then forsook
The black ravine, and with swift - moving feet,
Sped through the forest, where projecting rocks
And pathless thickets blocking up their path
Caused many a deviation. When they came
To a dark spot where the thick roof of leaves
Made night the blacker, lo !

    a sombre shape

Came creeping after them, and suddenly,
Loud crying, seized the monk, and sought with force
To snatch the sword that in his girdle hung.
Fiercely the monk fought, and the bandit bold
Fought to avenge his mates;—and thus they strove
Each to the death, thro' the thick underwood,
Now this one conquering and now that, until
Behind the trees they quite were lost to sight.
The maid, at first, in fear had fled, but then
Thoughts of her brother's danger, brought her back
To where she fled from. Here, with loud-raised cries,
She called her brother, wandering to and fro,
And searching brake and thicket, but in vain;
It seemed as though the earth had gulped them down.
Thus desperate, for hours, she wandering went
About the forest, till the breaking dawn

Shewed her a narrow path that led her steps
Out of the wood, to where the open cliff
Gave prospect clear and wide. Here at her feet
She saw a friendly village, through the mist,
Peeping a welcome. At the mountain's base
A clear deep stream, skirting the hamlet,
       flowed
Under a rustic bridge, that, white with rime,
Gleamed as with snow. The slowly-moving
       mists
Parted at last and the victorious sun,
Rising above the darkling forest-tops,

Hooded with golden rays a new-born world,
Awaking all to pleasure. In the boughs
Twittered the joyous birds, and blithely hailed
The happy morning light; but she, how oft,
Turning her sad face to the sombre wood,
Did then sigh forth her grief, that guileful fate
Had taken her brother almost ere it gave,
Had lied to her of happiness and joy,
And when her poor heart, listening to the charms
Of hope's false tale, had yielded to the dream
Of instant bliss,—then fate, with cruel hand,
Shaking her heart, had emptied it of joy,
And left it poorer, sadder, than before.

Now as her path lay by a little shrine,
She bowed her knees, and prayed, with burning soul,
Before the altar of the deity.
Meanwhile an old man, spade on shoulder, came

Along that way, and wondering saw the maid
Kneeling and groaning. Kindly drawing nigh,
He asked the cause of her fast-flowing tears.
But when the maid had told her mournful tale,
Deep pity seized him for her sad distress,
And strove to heal her grief with balm of words.
He led her to the village, where she dwelt,
As his own daughter, in his cottage home.
Girt round with palm-trees, in a sheltered spot,
Still and remote, the little cottage lay ;
From the trim garden, through a wooden gate,
A road led to the open, where the stream
Rushed valley-wards through rocks and boulders, thence
To the pine clad mountains. Driven by the wind,
The yellow leaves, chasing each other, fell
In little heaps beside the cottage door :
Half withered asters lay upon the floor,
And, with attenuated pipe, the choir
Of insects chirped its everlasting song.
With kindly heart and true paternal care,
The old man strove to cheat White Aster's grief,
That dwelt in silence on her loved ones lost.
Till soothed by tenderness, at last, she grew
To lose her sense of strangeness, and became
A grateful inmate of the peasants' house.

52

The year went by, and days and months again
Grew into years and vanished, as the foam
That crests the ocean's billows; as they passed,
White Aster bloomed to lovely womanhood,
And ofttimes in her simple village dress,
Passing through spring-clad fields, her beauty shone
Like to a branch of snow-white cherry-bloom,
Against the darkling screen of sombre pines.
Like pearls betwixt her lips, parted to smile,
Shone her white teeth, her fingers lithe and slim
Like pliant grass in springtime. Far and near
The country side rang with her beauty's praise,
And many a swain sighed when he heard her name;
Nay, even the Governor of the land had heard
White Aster's fame, and, hearing, had resolved
To seek her hand in marriage. So one day,
Following the custom of the land, he sent
An agent to the old man, to enquire
If he might have the maid. The simple man
Esteeming it an honour to the girl,
And fearing to offend so great a lord,

Gave glad consent.   Then, in the calendar,
After some short debate, they found a day
Propitious for the marriage; then he went
Back to his master, but the old man called
White Aster, and with joy upon his lips,
Trembling, related all that had occurred.
"In truth," quoth he, "it is an honour rare,
When one of noble lineage sends to woo
A peasant maid.   How could I miss a chance
That never might return?   The agent asked;
And I consented.   It is true you came
Seeking your father hither; but who knows
Whether he lives, or died long while ago?
This house has been to you a second home,
From which you must not wander forth again
To dim uncertainty,—now should you choose
A husband, that can guard your future life
From all mishap or danger.   Therefore, see
The index finger of Heaven's will in this,
And give consent to him as I consented."
But when White   Aster heard it, pale as Death,

And all as speechless sat she — then the tears
Broke from her eyes, her trembling breast's gan heave
And sink with grief, and answer gave she none;
The while the old man, all amazed, yet full
Of pity looked upon her.   Then at last
She broke her silence, and with weak voice said:
"Words of my poor dead mother, which she spoke,
Whilst yet my brother lived with us, remain
Firm fixed in my remembrance.   "Once," she said,
"Ere morn had scarce begun to dawn, I went
To worship at the temple: as I passed
Through the churchyard twixt rows of gravestones hoar,
And blooming white chrysanthemums, I heard
The piteous wailing of a little child.
Which following, I found, amidst the flowers,
A fair young child with crimson-mouthing lips,
And fresh soft cheeks — a veritable gem.
I took it as a gift that Buddha sent
As guerdon of my faith, and brought it up
As my own child, to be my husband's joy,
And mine: and as I found thee couched
Amidst white-blooming asters, I named thee
White Aster, in memorial of the day:
Thus are you Akihide's sister, and
His early playmate, and henceforth, you must

Practise all womanly accomplishments
And every maiden virtue, that you may,
In years to come be his true-hearted wife,"
Thus spake my mother then, and, since that time,
Though years have passed, and many a sad mishap
Has marred the hoped-for joy, my mother's words
Sound in my ears as clear, as though she stood
Bodily here before me.   I am bound
(My destiny all settled) till the dust

Claim back my earthly frame. These many years,
As thine own daughter thou hast nourished me,
And heartily I thank thee. My poor life,
Were that of service, would I offer for thee
In token of my lively gratitude. But this
Spare me, that I should be another's wife.
This, though it cost my life, I must refuse."
Thus weeping silently, she went and sat
Down in a corner: but the good old man
Anxious, and full of pain to break his word,
Sat doubting,—yet a secret hope remained
That haply yet her maiden heart might change.

Thinking of this and that, he sought what words
Of eloquence would win her, when the door
Opened, and lo! the agent, with a man
That dragged a heavy trunk, wherein were stored
The bridal gifts, which, with a sober air,
He spread to view upon the well-swept mats.
Silk garments, woven white, or gaily decked
With rich embroideries of varied hue,
Thin, that the wind in summer, blowing cool,
Could penetrate, or thick, with wadded warmth,
For winter days; sashes of gold brocade,
Sweet-scented coverlets, and rugs of fur,
That like new-fallen snow lay soft and white;
These and much else he took out piece, by piece,
From the great-bellied chest, till the quick words
Of admiration on the old man's lips

Died, and his gleaming eyes alone expressed
His pleasure. — But the neighbour's curious wife
Who, with a woman's mind, had followed in,

Upon the agent's heels, to see the gifts,
With unrestrained praise poured forth her words;
And, handling every gift, extolled the maid
That called such things her own. Street-children
          peep'd,
With wonder, thro' the hedge, their chubby hands
Pointing outstretched towards the magic gifts,

But poor White Aster, dumb with sorrow, sat
With drooping head and weeping bitterly.
Then, when the midnight darkness, covering, lay
Upon the silent fields, White Aster stole,
With silent-gliding footsteps, from the door;
And, though the wind blew chill upon her face,
And the night-loneliness struck to her heart,
Yet resolutely strode she to the stream,
Whose jasper-waves broke o'er the gleaming rocks.
Not by the trodden path, but through the grass,
And overhanging bushes, that no eye
Of man should mark her flight, nor the hard world
Know where, beneath the pall of darksome night,
She sought her tomb amidst the cold wet waves.

So came she to the bridge that spanned the
       stream,
Fast flowing 'neath its arch, and there her hands
Folded in prayer, and with heaven-glancing eye,
Repeated to herself the Sanskrit words
Which, as a child, she learned in Buddha's praise.
Then, stooping forward, stood in act to plunge
Into the cold deep stream, when, from behind,
A hand, firm-grasping, seized her by her robes,
And pulled her back. "Thanks be to Buddha,
       who,
Just at this hour, brought me to this dark spot
To save thee, silly child, from this rash deed.
For years, long years, I sought thee — now once
       more
I find thee — thus"! White Aster turned and looked
Her saviour in the face, incredulous:
Then, with a cry, fell on her brother's neck,
And sobbed forth her full heart in speechless joy.
But, when her tears had eased the pent up flood,
That pressed within her heart, at last her tongue
Was loosed and spoke. Ah! what a multitude

Of painful recollections had they both
To tell each other — all their sufferings,
And all their actions, since that cruel morn
When, scarce united, they were rent apart.
Meanwhile the moon's round face, with happy
        light,
Rose o'er the mountains — from the village rose
The unmelodious tones of rustic pipe;
Still they talked on; the quickly running hours
Passed in their course, and in the eastern sky
The pale dawn showed the face of coming day.
Then their straw shoes they tied secure and firm,
And with quick step began their homeward road,
If haply they could know their father's fate.
For weeks they wandered, and at last they came
To the old home.   The well - known plum
        trees stood
Within the smiling garden, and the gate
Of moss - grown bamboo stood to welcome them
Part of the house remained, surviving storms
Of wind, and civil war; the reed thatched roof,
Though broken, still gave shelter from the rain

With trembling heart Whiteaster pushed the gate
And entered — but what sight! an old man stood
Deep sunk in thought against an upright beam,
As counting the slow hours, impatiently,
Until that hoped - for children should come back.
Now he looks up! "Oh Father!"   Oh what joy
Breathes in that moment of a child's return!

  The sun retired to rest, the darkness fell,
And moon and stars kindled their nightly lamps.
The three sat joyful at the festive board;
For the old man welcomed with joy the son,
Whom once he drove to exile, praising much
His patience in misfortune; but his words
Came fastest when he praised the modesty
And virtue of the maid.   Then with a smile,
Uplifting high his brimming glass, he blessed
The hour that brought his children back to him,
After long painful absence; and enquired
Of their adventures, and himself began
To tell his own:

   "When on that morn I left
My home, and to the mountains bent my steps,
Making a slip, I lost my firm foothold,
And fell into a deep ravine.   In vain,
I tried a hundred dangerous roads

65

To scale the sheer sides of the hollow gorge,
That mocked my efforts; but wild berries grew
Abundantly for food, and in a hole
That scarcely covered me I slept at night.
But lo! one morning, as I gazed aloft,
Towards the o'erhanging cliffs, a monkey troop
Sat on a withered vine, and chattering
With cries, and wild grimaces, beckoned me.
I followed where they called, and seized the vine
That hung down to me, and, to my surprise,
It bore my weight, and so I came at last
To extricate myself; yet when I reached
The top, the troop had vanished without trace,

Only the crickets, chirping in the grass,
Filled all the mountain side with cheerful song.
Then came the thought that no blind chance had brought
The monkey-troop, and that my strange escape

Was caused by gratitude; for once it fell,
In winter - time, that as I hunted in the hills,
Amongst the snow, a female monkey sat
Holding her babe, beneath a tree.   I raised
My gun and aimed to shoot at her, but she
Began to cry, with such a human voice,
Praying for mercy, that my lifted gun
Sank harmless by my side.   I spared her life;
And she, in turn, seeing my sorry plight,
Cried to me from the rocks, and showed the way
To flee from certain death.   The silly beast
Knows how to show its gratitude, and shames
Many a thankless man.   For oh! how few,
In these degenerate days, remain to shew
True Faith and Honour, and unselfishly
To cling to duty! I alas! have fought
A rebel 'gainst my rightful lord and king,
Unmindful of my troth, and with black hands,
Wasted my fatherland.   Such men as I,
Unfaithful and ungrateful, stand below
The lower beasts.   Ah! when I recollect
All my base acts, my grieving heart is pierced
With pangs of penitence.   Your soul alone,
Whiteaster, still remains untouched and pure.
Only through you does my race still retain

Its costly gem of childlike faithfulness.
Wither the flowers in the gardens all,
The flower of thy heart shall wither ne'er."

RETURN HOME AT NIGHT.

T. INOUYE.

The clouds o'erveil
  The moon's pale face,
That shines above
  A king in space.

A sudden wail
  Fills all the air,
And whispering tones
  The wind-blasts bear.

The mighty pines
  Of sombre hue
Shudder, and lay
  Their heads askew,

Amidst the reeds
  The shadows glide
Like beckoning men
  Close by my side.

Where shades of night
    Fall on the plain,
I pass in fear
    A broken fane.

I cross the bridge
    By wooded hill,
And, homewards, seek
    The hamlet still

Long, long, hath passed
    The midnight hour:
No eye keeps watch
    In street or bower.

All sleep: no sound
    Comes on the breeze
Save where the owl
    Hoots in the trees.

MY BELOVED'S GRAVE.

M. UYEDA.

Vain was it
  All that I desired;
My beloved
  Was but a dream,
A fleeting, transient
  Ray of light.
And now my life
  Lies drear!

The solemn vow
  Betwixt us made
With faith unswerving
  Thou didst keep.
Though parents and kin
  Strove to make thee faithless.

Then slowly,
  Like a flower
That has no water,
  Thou didst droop.   And death
Came to thee as a welcome guest;
  For ev'n in death
Thou still art mine.

But when I heard
   That lone, all alone,
Thou hadst gone home,
   Leaving me, — then I knew
That in this life
   Objects of hope and love
Are not granted to man.

For thy sake,
   Seeking for distant lands,
I travelled far and near.
   For thy sake,
With toilsome labour sought I to obtain
   Wisdom's rich store.

See, see, now have I
   Come home again.
See, see, now am I
   Near to the wished-for goal;
But in vain
   Was all my fond endeavour.
Knowledge without love
   Is but a curse.

Crooked and cracked
    Stands thy poor tomb:
Evil weeds
    Grow round thy grave:
And the priest himself hath forgot
    The dead one's name!

Over the dry drear fields
    Autumn winds
Blow melancholy.
    Wait for me, love,
Under thy mossy stone;
    Soon shall I follow thee.

THE ONE WORD.

M. UYEDA.

He.   Ah! thus to love
        What grief it is!
    One word only,
        Dearest and Best!
    Whispering silently,
        Say that thou lovest me!

She.   When love is hidden
        It grows the best:
    Sorrow and pain
        Is this world's lot.
    In the world to come
        I'll whisper that word.

TO A DEPARTING LOVER.

When rain drops fall
  And wet your head;
Think that they are
  The tears I shed.

A DISAPPOINTMENT.

I dreamed that thou didst come to me,
   And laughing roused myself from sleep;
But when thy form I could not see,
   Joy fled, 'and I began to weep.

SMALLNESS OF THE WORLD.

How small the world has grown!
   Methinks that now
It cannot measure more than foar foot six.
For I, a humble man, scarce five foot tall,
   Find it impossible to fit myself
Into its small dimensions.

A CONDITIONAL GIFT.

Have thou no care for all the wealth
   That lies stored up in this fair earth;
For, if thou wilt, I can give thee
   All that the world contains of worth:
But only if thou promise me
   By day and night incessantly
To toil for it laboriously.

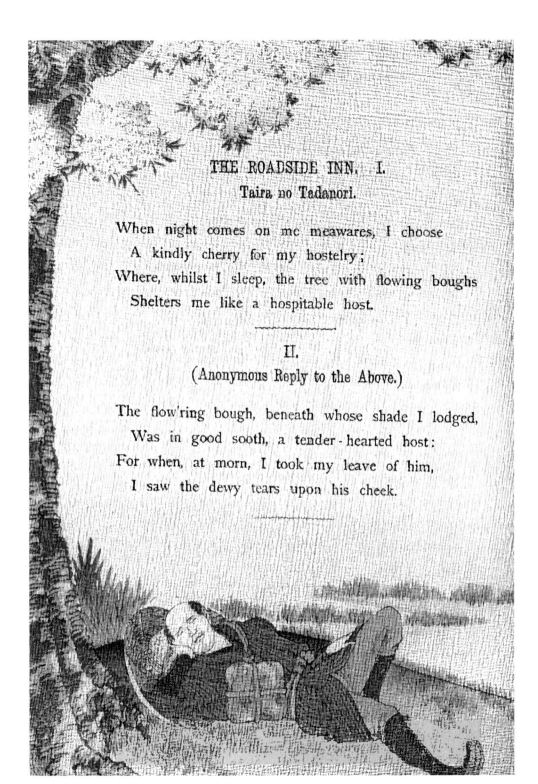

THE ROADSIDE INN. I.
Taira no Tadanori.

When night comes on me meawares, I choose
  A kindly cherry for my hostelry;
Where, whilst I sleep, the tree with flowing boughs
Shelters me like a hospitable host.

II.
(Anonymous Reply to the Above.)

The flow'ring bough, beneath whose shade I lodged,
  Was in good sooth, a tender-hearted host:
For when, at morn, I took my leave of him,
  I saw the dewy tears upon his cheek.

NOTES.

CANTO I.

p. 1. l. 3. **Aso - yama** an active volcano in the southern islands of Kyûshû.

p. 6. l. 6. **Mino,** rain - cloak made of straw.

p. 8. l. 3. When Japanese women cry they use the sleeves of their dresses as we do our pocket - handkerchiefs. The sleeves are generally lined with red silk.

p. 8. l. 10. The **Sutras** form one division of the Buddhist Scriptures.

p. 9. l. 1. Cemeteries are attached to most Buddhist Temples.

p. 9. l. 6. The windows (*Shoji*) of a Japanese house are sliding frames covered with white transparent paper.

p. 10. l. 9. The fox (*Kitsune*) plays a large part in Japanese popular superstition. It is supposed to be capable of assuming all kinds of shapes, and to play various tricks on people. It is therefore much feared.

p. 12. l. 8. **Si - shih** a celebrated Chinese beauty in the fifth century B. C. cf. Mayers, Chinese Reader's Manual. No. 571.

p. 13. l. 5. **Samurai,** the former warrior class in Japan.

p. 13. l. 6. The **Castle of Kumamoto** in Higo, Kyûshû, was formerly one of the strongest places in Japan, but is now in ruins. During the Satsuma Rebellion of 1877, which forms the historical background of this poem, and especially of White Aster's narrative, it was besieged in vain

79

by the rebel general **Saigō Takamori.** The last battle between Saigo and the victorious government troops took place on the 24th September 1877 on Shirayama ("White Mountain") near Kagoshima. Here Saigo met his death. For further notices of the rebellion see Rein's Japan, Eng. Ed. p. 372-375.

p. 14. l. 2. **Sudare.** Light curtains made of thin bamboo.

p. 14. l. 20. Kumamoto, threatened by the approaching rebels.

CANTO II.

p. 29. l. 9. The Province of **Hōshū** or **Bungo** lies S. W. of Higo.

p. 34. l. 4. The **Koto** is a kind of zither, generally with 13 strings.

p. 35. l. 10. The **Siang** is a tributary of the Yang-tsze-kiang in China, and is famous for the bamboos growing in its district.

p. 35. l. 15. This and the following lines are reminiscences from Chinese Mythology.

p. 38. l. 18. **Yedo,** — now Tokyo (since 1868), capital of Japan.

p. 38. l. 20. **Kei-u,** the literary name of the celebrated sinologue **Nakamura,** who died a few years ago.

p. 38. l. 21. Here are meant the old Chinese Classics, i. e. the moralists; and The Scriptures of Buddhism.

p. 44. l. 13. It is a popular belief that wild geese commence their flights at a regular hour, so that their appearance may serve as a note of time.

CANTO III.

p. 52. l. 18. All marriages in Japan are treated as family rather than as individual affairs, and are arranged by a go-between (**Nakōdo**).

p. 53. l. 3. In Japan, as in China, "auspicious days" are chosen for the commencement of any important undertaking. They are marked in the calendars.

p. 55. l. 3. Marriages between adopted brothers and sisters are allowed, and, under certain circumstances, common. In a family where there is only one son or one daughter, a child of opposite sex is often adopted with a view to an eventual marriage. The adopted son takes the family name, and in this way the name (so important in Japanese eyes) is saved from extinction.

p. 57. l. 5. The betrothal is considered to be ratified by the interchange of bridal gifts (the kind and number of which is fixed by custom for all classes). After such ratification, the betrothal cannot be broken off, except by mutual consent of both families.

p. 60. l. 14. White Aster meditates suicide in accordance with a well-established Japanese code of honour.

p. 62. l. 4. There are to be found in Japanese Buddhism several corrupted Sanskrit or Prakrit formulae, such as **Namu Amida Butsu.** (Glory to the Infinite Buddha) and **Giate, giate, hara giate, hara so giate, so wa ka.** (Corruption of the Sanskrit words *Gate gate pāragate pārasam-gate bodhi svāhā* "O wisdom, gone, gone, gone to the other shore, landed on the other shore, Svāha!" which form the closing words of the shorter Prajñā-Pāramitā-Hridaya-Sûtra). The Chinese equivalents however are often used.

p. 70. The **Return Home at Night**, like White Aster (by the same author) is written in Chinese, and appeared in the author's collection entitled . . . . .

p. 72. 75. The two poems by Prof. Uyeda (Imperial University, Tokyo) are so-called **Shin-tai-shi**, new style poems. For these see Dr. Florenz on "Modern Japanese Literature" in fasciculus 47 of the Mittheilungen der deutschen Gesellschaft für Natur- and Völkerkunde Ostasiens.

p. 76-77. So-called **Dodoitsu**, popular poems, generally anonymous.

ERRATA.

p. 6. l. 6. **straw cloak** for **blue cloak**.

p. 18. l. 12. **taught** for **thought**.

p. 22. l. 12. A quotation mark (") is to be inserted at the end of the line.

p. 35. l. 4. **trees** for **tress**.

p. 50. l. 25. **peasant's** for **peasants'**.

p. 53. l. 2. An apostrophe (') in **breast's** is to be deleted.

p. 64. l. 1. and p. 68. l. 24. **White Aster** for **Whiteaster**.

p. 73. l. 9. **far** for **for**.

Errata in the numeration of the page.................51 for 52.

    „   „   „   „   „   „   „ -----------------53 for 54.

有 所 權 版

LIST OF BOOKS OF CREPE PAPER.

POETICAL GREETINGS FROM THE FAR EAST:
JAPANESE POEMS.

FREELY RENDERED FROM THE GERMAN OF

PROF. DR. K. FLORENZ, BY REV. A. LLOYD, M.A.

Japanese Fairy Tale Series :

No. 1-20 ; 20 Pamphlets in a neat box.
„ 21 Three Reflections.
„ 22 The Flowers of Remembrance and Forgetfulness.
„ 23 The Goblin Spider.
Oyuchasan.
Kohanasan.
Princess Splendor.
The Children's Japan.
Japanese Topsyturvydom.
Japanese Pictures of Japanese Life.

&c. &c. &c.

T. HASEGAWA,
PUBLISHER & ART-PRINTER,
10 HIYOSHIOHO, TOKYO.

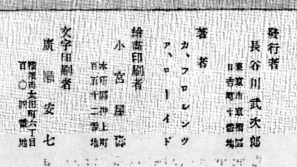

明治三十年十二月一日印刷
同年十二月十日發行

發行者
長谷川武次郎
東京市京橋區
日吉町七番地

著者
カ、フロレンツ
ア、ロイド

捺搣印刷者
小宮屋善七
本所區十二柳上町

文字印刷者
廣瀬安七
横濱南太田町六丁目
〇四百番地